THE FIRST MIRACLE IS THE BOOK ITSELF...

"LAUREL LEE HAS SUCH A CLEAR WAY OF 'TELLING IT AS IT WAS,' that I often felt as if I were rooming with her in the hospital ward! She shows us that humor can be real medicine in times when we all walk through our own fires. She is super!"

—Joni Eareckson,
Author of *Joni*

"My wife and I were both helped by Laurel Lee's book. We who are older need to be reminded and encouraged to have simple faith and to be glad in the Lord in difficult times as well as easier days. Laurel Lee has done this for us."

—Dr. Ken Taylor,
Translator of *The Living Bible*

"Laurel Lee needed to say very little about her practical walk with Jesus Christ. It shouts from every page! In fact, reading *Walking Through the Fire* was more than reading an absorbing book. It was an experience in the indisputable life—today—of Jesus Christ Himself. I see no other way in which she could have endured as she did and come out 'flying.'"

—Eugenia Price

WALKING THROUGH THE FIRE

A Hospital Journal

BY LAUREL LEE

Illustrated with drawings
by the author

BANTAM BOOKS
TORONTO · NEW YORK · LONDON

WALKING THROUGH THE FIRE
*A Bantam Book / published by arrangement with
E. P. Dutton & Company, Inc.*

PRINTING HISTORY
*Dutton edition published May 1977
3 printings through June 1978*
A selection of The Literary Guild November 1977
Serialized in United Feature Syndicate October 1977
Bantam edition / July 1978
2nd printing
3rd printing
4th printing
5th printing

Back cover photograph by Dr. Stu Levy

ISBN 0-553-11430-1

Published simultaneously in the United States and Canada

*Bantam Books are published by Bantam Books, Inc. Its trade-
mark, consisting of the words "Bantam Books" and the por-
trayal of a bantam, is registered in the United States Patent
Office and in other countries. Marca Registrada. Bantam
Books, Inc., 666 Fifth Avenue, New York, New York 10019.*

PRINTED IN THE UNITED STATES OF AMERICA

To my father, James Moore,
and my mother, Ruth Moore;

"Honor thy father and mother,
that thy days may be long upon the land."

And to my brothers and sisters who have been,
and will be.

When thou walkest through the fire,
thou shall not be burned,
neither shall the flame be kindled upon thee.

ISAIAH 43:2

In my palm was a handful of cards.
"Look doctor," I said, "let's read
them together." The favored one
read "pregnant" while the others
said "anemia" and "cough." I didn't
know what a long game it was going
to be and just how stacked was the deck . . .

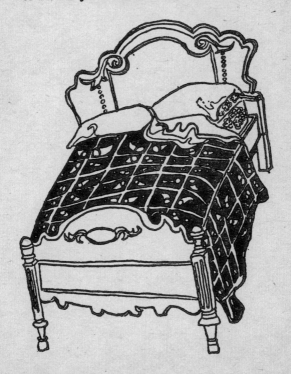

The family practice clinic is located in a separate building within the multiservice cluster of the University of Oregon Medical School. One physician cares for the medical problems of the entire family unit. For my prenatal care, I was assigned to Dr. Michael Mainer, who was in his third year of residency.

Once a month I would ride the bus to Emma Jones Hall at the top of the hill. Once a month Dr. Mainer would record the early prenatal questions and answers.

He was a number genius. My weight was the first data of his inquiry. He could remember my previous scores without the chart, as if he were a collector of fat-lady baseball cards.

He chided me the month I splurged on peanut butter cookies.

"Oh, it's my hiking boots," I said, clicking my heels together.

"Well, maybe," he answered.

After each visit the children and I would eat a picnic in the forest behind the building, and once we built a fort.

Sometimes medical students also would bring their lunch bags into the sunshine. I would listen to their conversation. All they seemed to talk about was who among their classmates and teaching staff smoked cigarettes.

I did not know if I were young and they were old or if I were old and they were young.

Also in the world at this time was a man who made certain powerful additions to his motorcycle and with a parachute and a great deal of publicity intended to jump the Snake River Canyon. He crashed, but lived. The same week I had my own cycle adventure. My son balanced on my bicycle crossbar. It was the most expedient way to go to the grocery store. What I gained in speed was a haste that made waste. It was a study of gravity. The bike went down the hill. Matthew's boot gravitated to the spokes. The obstruction abruptly halted all speed. Matthew jumped and escaped our collapse, but the accident caused my knee to swell. I went to the doctor and had my first X ray and rode in my first wheelchair. My knee was fine but I was miserable that my bike was broken.

Every night I experienced a phenomenon that I regarded as a mystery of my pregnancy. As soon as I slept I would perspire until the discomfort of my wet nightclothes would wake me. My body could produce such an abundance of water in the night sweat I thought I was turning into a mermaid, but could not complete the chemistry.

the night was
a long passage
to light.

There was a cold.
In the middle of the cold
There was a cough.
It never went away,
But came to stay.

The cough always wanted to be heard:

"I will not cough," I said, and counted
as long as I could. The COUGH won.

"I will hold my breath," I said.
But the COUGH won.

"I will suck green cough-killer drops," I said.
But the COUGH won again.

Friday—October 3, 1975

When the cough coughed all night I went up on
the hill again. Dr. Mainer pulled up on his bicycle just as I arrived at the door. "I'm sick," I
said, and he told me to get a chest X ray.

"No. I'm pregnant and X rays aren't good. Anyway, I don't smoke cigarettes and nothing is that serious."

He listened, but did not waver. He said, "I'm going that way," and walked me to the X-ray department. He told me to bring my X rays back to the clinic. We stepped into an elevator and Dr. Mainer introduced me to Dr. Stu Levy, who operated the elevator buttons as if we were all in a department store, calling out the merchandise on each floor:

"PHOTOGRAPHIC EQUIPMENT,
PHOTOGRAPHY
NUMBER 3"

I walked out with Matthew and Anna following me like puppies. The technicians shielded me with a lead apron over a white gown. When I was dressed, they asked to do another view and they wouldn't let me take my X rays to the family practice office. I was heavy inside, as if I were still wearing their shield. Even the air felt dense in the waiting room.

The kingdom of my two children tap-danced through the day. Wonder lay at their every corner:

Imagine seeing a machine that takes pictures of the inside of bodies.

Imagine seeing real pictures of real bones on real lighted screens.

They lay on the floor and watched the old Otis elevator with all its cables go up and down.

I was called to the examining room and sat under one of the bright posters that bright doctors' offices always seem to have.

"What does the sign say, Mother?"

"Oh, that is true!" (Matthew, age 5).

The doctors' faces were a professional grim. The one with Dr. Mainer was from surgery, a doctor I never saw again. He indicated to me my very own bone poster, with an extra white sac hanging next to the lung. He brought in those first enrollment papers of my family's medical history and asked about the notation of cancer on my mother's side.

He asked how many children I had, and indicated a real concern about my pregnancy, now starting its sixth month. As they examined me the doctors exchanged, with their eyes, their verification of swollen lymph nodes in my neck. They talked their serious talk in the hall, and I could hear them when my childrens' chattering permitted me. I could hear the word *tumor*.

I was full of plans for the future, like a tree of leaves. They fell off the branches at once, not blowing away, but laid at the root.

I was in myself, receiving a new dimension of concerns, and I was outside myself, watching myself receive it. I was not upset, and I puzzled at this:

When it rains all winter and our house shrinks to where my outstretched arms can touch the walls; I run outside and shout at the hedge "HOW MANY PEOPLE CAN WE FIT IN A PHONE BOOTH?"

When the children both cry at once, demand at once, fight at once, and break at once; then the violin strings in my mind snap, and I have no melody.

When Richard walks through the house, his head turning into a growling bear, I faint away inside.

I called Richard from the hall phone, outlining the events of the day and the pending hospitalization the following Monday.

I walked outside thinking, "I get to think about things that usually would be held from me until later seasons of life. Wisdom is the principal thing." My body rode the bus home, and I executed the correct mechanical procedures to transport us, but my mind kept sorting images.

My experience that Friday encompassed six hours at the doctor's office. That night I had a

strange dream: A photographer had come to take yearbook pictures at the clinic, and all the staff formed in lines on the steps of Emma Jones Hall—lines of doctors smiling. Then someone said, "She's been here so long, include her in the shot." Thus, we were all recorded in black and white.

Saturday—October 4, 1975

The doctors were too serious for me not to be serious. I made an appointment within myself to consider dying. I wanted to look in the face of death, sit on its lap and smell its breath.

I had seen life as an ongoing stream that I was just immersed in. I always felt that its path would take me to the outermost parts of the earth. Portland was only a temporary camping spot for the nurture of young children. In one stroke I cut with some mental shears that fifty-more-year river, leaving me a short stretch.

I cried. I wept sore. I wanted the privilege of guiding the arrows of my children and giving them the wisdom that could shoot them into the high place.

I was melancholy. My memory pulled out special days and old ways that had had their fragrance.

Even the meditation of death progresses: It was like a dark glass I had to pass through. Death is the last enemy.

Music came. Chorus and voices, in tones and scales, in patterns and textures, repeating a joyous sound.

"He who liveth and believeth in Me shall not die, but have everlasting life." JESUS CHRIST

I was free. I felt I could fly around the room. I knew it would all have to be faced again; some more black-and-white runs, and once in living color.

HOSPITAL
OCT. 6

I had never really been in a hospital before, except to walk in and out with a new baby.

After being admitted and issued a plastic bag of necessities (including toilet paper), I was delivered to a bed.

There was a voice in the ceiling out in the hall that spent its days and nights calling doctors' names.

I landed in another planet, and suffered from some manifestation of cultural shock.

My first morning found a group of family practice doctors clustered by my bed. Dr. Mainer made his introductory remark: "This patient weighs one hundred and sixty pounds."

I felt instantly reduced to a county fair 4-H

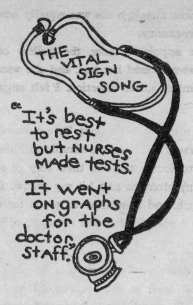

THE VITAL SIGN SONG

"It's best to rest but nurses made tests.

It went on graphs for the doctor staff."

Club entry. I was not silent as a sheep before my shearers, but with a touch of sarcasm repeated: "Yes, this patient weighs one hundred and sixty pounds." Then I was so embarrassed; I wanted them to just go away. One by one they felt my swollen lymph nodes. Then they left to complete their rounds.

When I was first introduced to my chest X ray, the doctor had said, "This presents certain ethical considerations in regard to the pregnancy." From that time I knew the baby was threatened. It was ironic that my first roommate had come for an abortion, although she was equally advanced in her pregnancy.

At an appointed hour, the yellow curtains were drawn around her bed, and she was given an abdominal saline injection. I felt anguish.

I had my own recreations. Two doctors, aided by a nurse, came to get a sample of bone marrow. I studiously avoided their tray of tools. I lay on my stomach and bit my pillow. It hurt very much, and it seemed to go on for a long time. So I pretended it was the days of the Inquisition. I was being tortured for Truth, and I would not accept deliverance. Later, their excavation site hurt no more, but my jaw ached from biting the pillow.

That night at eleven o'clock, I met the surgeon, Dr. Hood. He was elected to biopsy a lymph node, and thus we would know my malady. I asked him to share with me the possible ramifications of the tumor. It was like he took a deck of cards called "Great Infirmities" out of his pocket and laid them before me:

INFIRMITY

| Cancer of the lung | Hodg-kin's disease | Cancer of lymphoid tissue | Leu-kemia | Tuber-culosis |

He left me with an assignment: to scrub the left side of my neck with betadine, an antiseptic solution. I thought the right side might not look clean by contrast so I scrubbed my whole neck.

This was repeated in the morning, on the left side, by a nurse.

A stretcher came for me. Because of my pregnancy, I was allowed no narcotics to make it a twilight journey.

I was humming a little brave tune, but I was really overcome by the strangeness of the surgery corridor. The orderly seemed to step on a button, and *whoosh*, the doors opened into an odd country inhabited by people in green hats and baggy green shoes.

Before I could enter into my own surgery room, there seemed to be another admission form to fill out in addition to my signed consent slip. My identity was made verbally, then by hospital wristband, and operation schedule. I was asked a string of questions.

1. "Have your dentures been removed?"
   "I don't have any."
   We progressed to number ten. Allergies.
   "Do you really care if I'm allergic to dust and cat hair?"

But that was dutifully recorded.

After all the betadine preparations on the left side of my neck, Dr. Hood, without any obvious examination, had the nurse scrub the right side and cover me with sterile cloths. They covered my head and I could not see. As they began their incision, they laid their tools on my face. I didn't think I was going to be able to handle it, until words came to me like a standard in my mind:

> That which is seen will pass away,
> that which is not seen is eternal.

The conversation in the surgery room seemed so ludicrous; the nurses were talking about the cost of their new shoes. I was returned to my room feeling as if they had left a small tool inside my neck.

My next hurdle was waiting the days until the pathology report was complete. I found that the day shift lived by "proper procedure," and there were established guardians of rules and regulations. But the night shift was free, indeed. To some degree, I inverted my schedule: sleeping, as permitted, by day, and up at night.

The head night nurse gave me my chart to study, and I pored over all the comments and suggestions of what my illness might be. "Hodgkin's disease" was the most frequent notation, so I began to gather and learn all that I could, although my resources were limited to the floor library. I found a medical journal that outlined the indications of the disease's spread: the stages, the cell-type categories, and an outline of treatment. The article had two quotations which I memorized:

1. Pregnancy does not seem to affect the course of the disease.
2. The disease doesn't have any known effect on fertility, pregnancy, or on the children conceived by a parent with Hodgkin's disease.

I frequently did my reading in a doctor's anteroom, and there I had a confrontation with a young resident. He rebuked me for my study. He told me to stick to articles I could understand, like those in *Reader's Digest*. I wasn't even tolerant; I voted him Creep of the Week.

One morning during the family practice rounds, I told the doctors all I had learned about Hodgkin's, feeling like I was giving a talk to a college science class.

That afternoon, Dr. Hood came to see me. He had just received the laboratory report. He held my hand while telling me I had nodular-sclerosing Hodgkin's disease. He suggested I begin aggressive radiation therapy as soon as possible. But before the therapy began, it would be best, he stated, to have an abortion. I couldn't even consider an abortion, even with all his persuasive logic.

Later, Dr. Mainer came in with the same news. I told him that really I had been the very first to know.

The stitches were removed from my neck, and I was issued some medication because of a hazy urine culture. A nurse explained how this medication could cross the placental barrier. So I buried the pills in my hospital plants, and after I was discharged I let them rest unused in my home medicine chest.

2

HOSPITAL
OCT. 12

We learn obedience by the things that we suffer.
On October 12, Sunday afternoon, I was re-admitted through emergency with severe abdominal pain.

Sunday is not a day for doctors; Dr. Mainer had to come, just because of my call. Upon examination he said, "You have a rip-roaring urinary-tract infection." He asked if I had taken my prescription.

Oh, humble moment.

He could have yelled, pushed me off the table, and told me what he had once planned for Sunday. But he exhibited true mercy. From that time, I always took my medication.

My outline for Monday was to go to ultrasound, a department where the gestational age of the baby could be indicated. But their equipment was temporarily out of order, so I was taken first to the radiation department. I was terrified. I felt I was being pushed in a little cattle car to Auschwitz, or some other extermination camp.

My fears all came upon me when I saw the corridor. I have never had an understanding of machines, small or great. Patients were treated behind lead-lined doors that read:

Red lights were turned on while technicians turned knobs, watching the cancer victims on TV screens.

I was taken into an examination room. I prayed with utter fervor. There I had a vision in which my mind could see a story:

> Naman was a Syrian who had leprosy. He sought a prophet of God who told him to dip seven times in the Jordan river, and he would be whole. Naman balked at the word; but he obeyed and was well.

There was much more than this, but it was clear to me that I had a course to follow, and in my submission to radiation, I would be restored.

I could face the staff with calmness. The plan was to start radiation treatments in what they called the high mediastinal field, delivering two thousand rads over a period of two and a half weeks.

It was still not an easy assignment. I was placed under an enormous cobalt machine. My imagination turned loose to a modern episode in *The Perils of Pauline*, an approaching science-fiction torment. I was alone and at war with my meditation.

Can one know my joy when the technicians returned with Dr. Mainer, halting the procedure until the ultrasound diagnosis was complete?

I jumped off the table, hopped on one foot, clapped my hands, refused the wheelchair transportation service, and went my way rejoicing.

I was interrupted at dinner, when a transportation-service orderly came to take me to ultrasound. There I lay on a cot as they covered my abdomen with oil, and with a gliding tool etched the infant within me on a screen. Their measurement estimated the gestational age at thirty-two weeks, in contrast to my own twenty-seven week calculation.

Because of the acceleration of the due-date, the therapeutic decision was now to postpone radiation until the baby was born. I was discharged with a pending follow-up appointment in the high-risk pregnancy clinic.

I was sick at home, but my family surrounded me. Our house is so small, I can be in bed and look into every room but one. So even in bed, I was in the bosom of my family.

Our agreement in marriage had always held to a strict division of labor. Richard did the man things, and I did the woman things, without crossing our streams. By necessity, Richard had begun to clean our house and cook our food. With great amazement, I rested on the couch and watched him cook dinner. Anything in life seemed possible. That was like turning the course of mighty rivers with a bare hand.

He had always been good with the children, but he increased in that capacity too. I would strain my ears to hear his bedtime serial stories of sailing ships, walking sticks, and trains. Bedtime was more than what had been my hasty guidance through toothbrush hygiene, so we were all enriched.

My symptoms got progressively worse. Night sweats drenched me. I was so short of breath that I could not read aloud, and I could hardly sing. Still, I coughed, although "Red Bomb," my

cough syrup, reduced the rack of it to lower-case letters. Going to the doctor was my chorus; it repeated itself after every verse in my life.

During one visit to the clinic I was asked if I would make a videotape in the basement of Emma Jones Hall.

I had been feeling like a soap-opera star through all the suspended decisions. I could hum violin music, look at the wall, and invite every-one to tune in again tomorrow.

I asked the nurse about the tape. She replied, "It will probably be used in the death-and-dying series in the nursing and medical school studies."

"Oh," I answered, sobered.

The day of the taping Dr. Mainer took me down the stairs into an illuminated room.

I sat in a news-room chair across from a pleasant-seeming man whose gray hair was crew-cut. When the interview started he changed before me into a machine that ejected hard balls for me to bat answers back to. It was alive with high fastballs and curves. My inquirer was without mercy. He kept my mind swinging.

Finally he said, "Is there anything you would like to know?"

"Yes. Who are you?" I asked.

He was the kind who answers questions with questions. "Who have you heard that I am?"

"Dr. Tollhouse," I said.

"That is close," said Dr. Taubman.

Later Dr. Mainer explained that he was the staff psychiatrist.

Then I had perfect understanding of why the world calls them "shrinks." My brain collapsed the rest of the day from his probing.

He seemed ever-learning and never-understanding.

I followed my appointment in the OB clinic with Dr. Montoya, the chief resident. He looked like a pizza baron. He wore a tomato-sauce tie. He threw his words up and out, baking everything with the intensity of his expression. He went through every progressing abdominal measurement and date and concluded ultrasound was right. I had a little calendar that marked my last period, which would still put me in the six-month chute. I spoke what I felt was true, but I felt more concerned for the baby than myself. Thus, I was relieved when Dr. Montoya confirmed that they would use a drug to induce labor as soon as the infant had sufficiently matured. This induction would supersede radiation therapy.

I was also seeing Dr. Mainer, who agreed with my calculations, but we flowed with the more expert opinion. I had weekly chest X rays which showed that the tumor was enlarging, and the lymph nodes were increasing in size.

As much as I thrilled to Richard's help, there was one drawback. He didn't cook with a great repertoire. For breakfast we always had very hard eggs; the yolk could support a fork in a vertical position. This was accompanied by a helping of pork and beans. Dinner was mostly hamburgers with very boiled vegetables and a lettuce wedge.

I began to lose my appetite and thought it was a symptom of progressive disease. Then one day I just didn't feel like swallowing any more.

I shared this with Dr. Mainer by telephone. He said, "This is worrisome."

LAUREL'S $20.00 STOVE

3

HOSPITAL
OCT· 31

Following Dr. Mainer's orders, I was admitted into the hospital that same Friday night. Dr. Steve Fredrickson was on call. I had never met him, but was advised he would be my weekend attending physician.

He came into the room, and I said, "You must be Dr. Fredrickson."

He said, "Just call me Steve."

It usually takes so long for a doctor to drop his occupational manner with a patient, and share anything personal. But Steve was first a person, and used the doctors' vocabulary only when relevant. I noticed another thing too: He was the first doctor whose classic black bag was not embossed with his title in gold letters. Personalness removes strangeness, and is a comfort.

A patient is continually exposed to groups of medical students and department specialists. I found I could classify doctors into three styles of patient management:

1. The doctor who shares only the very immediate: that present moment.
2. The doctor who shares the next step, and explains in some detail its construction.
3. The doctor who points to the vast landscape ahead, showing not only bridges and cities but every possible avenue.

There are always exceptions. I had one fourth-year student from hematology who told me glibly I had five years to live. I could laugh at him because I knew my disease and knew I knew more about it than he did. I had continued to study Hodgkin's disease, reading from books and current journals to protect myself from every wind and doctrine of doctors. I also wanted more understanding to refute my imaginings when I felt so sick and fading.

This was my third time in the hospital. In addition to the other symptoms, my admittance sheet stated: "Onset of dysphagia." The progress report was more graphic: "Today intake has been minimal, but patient noticed difficulty in swallowing, with sensation of food becoming 'hung-up' in throat."

I was scheduled for a barium swallow to see if the tumor was affecting my esophagus. Simulta-

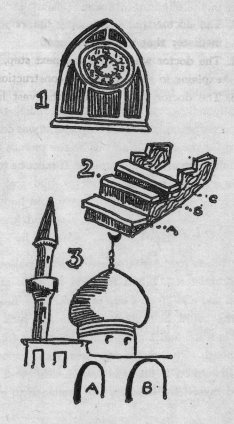

neously, the nurses made summaries on their page: ". . . complained of being hungry. . . ." Another noted ". . . ate well at breakfast and lunch, requested double orders."

I realized it was Richard's cooking that had precipitated my hospitalization. I felt trapped, forced to walk through yet another bull ring. The humor of the circumstance was apparent to me too. I wadded the ludicrousness of it up and stuffed it in my hospital-gown pocket.

I continued to make primitive observations. The surgeon wanted to abort, the radiologist wanted radiation, and the OB specialist was concerned for the infant. Can this be the essence of the multidisciplinarian approach? It must be too simple a generalization.

November 1, Saturday

I was taken to the site where barium swallows are administered. I had to stand between machines, and was given a cup of thick, white fluid. Nothing could have prepared me for such a horrible-taste, and I gagged and spewed it from my mouth. The technician was very serious when he asked if this was how I swallowed. I braced myself for the cup, and managed to get

ASHES
ASHES
WE ALL FALL DOWN

the barium down. There was little evidence of obstruction.

I was transferred to the OB floor, where there were a number of women with high-risk pregnancies. But the majority were young mothers who would come and go. There was such evidence of joy among the delivered citizens. I was always sighing within myself that everything would go well for me.

It was a terrible way to spend a Sunday morning. I was transported to diagnostic ultrasound, where their etching device located a pocket of amniotic fluid. By extracting a sample of this water, the lab could determine the maturity of the fetal lungs.

The package of tools for the tap looked medieval. I felt like a picture in a sequence of the history of medicine. But wherever you are, there you are, and it was done.

The lab report was returned, marked "immature." Examination determined the fetal size to be a mere four pounds.

Somehow Dr. Mainer had begun to concur with Dr. Montoya that the gestational age was now thirty-five weeks. I knew it was thirty weeks and even argued with Dr. Montoya in a dream.

Ambassadors from all the specialized countries of medicine came to see me and to examine my culture with their varied proposals of aid. They had a United Nations meeting to decide my governing treatment policies. Delegates came from hematology, neonatal pediatrics, family practice, and the OB service. They were moving to the conference room. I felt it was my right to go.

From an access closet by the delivery corridor I removed a full doctor's outfit and dressed myself, disguising the bulk of Laurel into what I hoped looked like another doctor who could deliver a baby. Only my eyes showed through the headgear. I planned to grab a metal chart board and hang around the door.

Alas, Dr. Montoya found me touching up the last of my costume. He sent me soundly to bed. He said, "You can't go because we yell at these meetings." And I bet they take off their shoes and pound them too.

The hematology staff chief had given me a bedside discourse. At the conclusion of his talk he asked his colleague, Dr. Bagby, to share his perceptions with the group: "Immediate radiation therapy is required as further encroachment on the superior vena cava will endanger the life of the mother and the fetus . . ."

When we were little children, we played a little game called "telephone." We would sit in a circle. One would whisper some news to the one next to him. And around and around would this little word be passed until the last to receive it would speak what he heard. We would laugh at how it had been jumbled.

The progression of the hematologist's words from my bedside to the group, through Dr. Montoya, and back to me varied not in one jot or phrase. I was not ignorant of the danger of radiation to the fetus. Dr. Montoya had been emphatic about the chance of retardation.

Tears just welled in my eyes, and that was another heavy little corner in the afternoon at the medical school.

November 4

I girded my mind and went to radiation therapy. They were unable to obtain my progressive X rays, and no one from radiation therapy had been able to attend the conference. A staff member examined me and stated he was not convinced I was really in need of radiation. In consideration of the pending due-date, he felt that the decision to initiate therapy was completely mine, and I should consider it well.

Transportation was called and I was returned to my room.

I was in real stress. All men were liars. If I had had any strength, I would have run away for the afternoon just to look at one solid thing, like a tree.

They called for me again. They had located my X rays. Those pictures had crossed out all the radiologist's morning words. The radiation began at once. The betatron machine was chosen, because it emitted the least scatter.

I was rolled under its girth. Earphones were applied because the machine roared as it worked. They put small rice bags on my neck, and a lead apron over my abdomen. I could feel the baby moving within me and my mind was held constant to God.

The day of the second treatment, peace of mind rolled slowly back up and filled me. I spent the hours of that returning tide with my water colors, painting a little picture. I recalled the lines from Isaiah:

When thou walkest through the fire,
thou shall not be burned,
neither shall the flame be kindled upon thee.

My days lay in bed, except for the radiation call.

I cranked the hospital cot up as high as it would go, to give my eye the best of the panorama from my window. I watched the movement of the city and the progression of the sky. Sometimes boats pulled logs, bound in chains, up the Willamette River. It was a provision for my spirit.

"WHEN THOU WALKEST THROUGH THE FIRE, THOU SHALT NOT BE BURNED, NEITHER SHALL THE FLAME BE KINDLED UPON THEE." ISAIAH 43:2

The nurse's note read: "Patient prefers to have bed all the way up. Refuses to let me roll it down. Climbs in and out of bed with help of chair. Was told how dangerous this was. R.N. Notified."

On the second floor the nurses' notes hung at the end of the bed. But the OB floor policy was to enclose them in an inaccessible chart. I found if a nurse was conscious that the notes were available to the patient, it produced one kind of recording of physical movements. The notations tucked within a chart held at the desk were another style, often dealing with their perception of the patient's emotional realm.

I found what seemed like tender concern from a nurse would elicit my tender confidence, only to find it distorted and recorded for the hospital world. I felt betrayed and limited their probes to the external.

Some notes made me sound a little insane: "At 0500 still awake and ravenously eating an orange—short of breath . . . no complaints." Another: "Poor breakfast. States, 'Not hungry,' had milk and juice. Saves food from the trays and places on window ledge and in drawer. States, 'Hate to waste food.'"

The OB floor could swarm with a great influx, until they would even put patients in the supply room. One Friday the rooms were crowded with extra beds.

I prevailed upon Dr. Mainer for a weekend pass. I had missed my little children so greatly. In my transportation to radiation, I would ride through the outpatient pediatric clinic and ache through that track, seeing the small faces.

I went home and we were all precious together. Everything had so much color. Richard kept our old wood stove so stocked with lumber

that the corner of the house was of a tropical warmth.

Matthew found in a plastic bag of fruit one more mottled than the rest. "Look Mom, it's got Hodgkin's disease."

Anna is only three. She would climb on my lap, dragging my old yellow bathrobe, rubbing its nylon lining and sucking her fingers.

In its sweetness was a sadness too. I felt I was carrying an hourglass of our fleeting time together. I dragged my feet all the way back to the hospital.

My roommate of the previous week had had a cold, and I had breathed in her sneezes. At home what was tropical by night was arctic by morning. By Tuesday, November 11, I had bronchitis. I had severe chest pain which warred against my cough center:

"I must cough" versus "No, that's real pain."
As they locked in combat;
I couldn't even breathe ...

The tumor was swelling from radiation in its own death process, and I had great shortness of breath. They hung an oxygen water-fountain box above my bed. They fastened this pure air into me with nose prongs. I kept thinking, if the urban air pollution continues, we'll all be wearing some kind of portable unit in a few years.

A university hospital is a learning institution, where the young students are reared to become old and wise doctors. Dr. Bagby brought a class of students into my room. He had me sit in a chair. He moved a stethoscope across my back and had me continually pronounce the letter *E*. As I understood him, he was explaining how this letter *E* would sound like the letter *A* as it crossed the chest mass.

Then it was the students' turn. One by one, I continually made the letter *E* for them. I blew *E*s out in the air. I became hysterical in my imagination. I felt we were making a tape for a preschool show on the alphabet. I thought I turned into a Cheshire cat, and that was all I could say. I couldn't bear the absurdity and began to say, in the same tone of voice, the letter *A*. No one even noticed. We had all gone insane.

Doctors and patients are at two elevations. I knew everyone by their belt buckles. They were subtle, midline bumper stickers. I read them in profusion.

There was the grass roots category with metal marijuana leaves. Mike Mainer wore a stylized eagle. One doctor friend had a Mickey Mouse head. It seemed that the minority had simple squares, just functional, without a style.

I was always meeting new doctors. Dr. Leslie Dillow came into my room reading my chart. After some study she asked, "Didn't it hurt to turn thirty?" I was so used to objective questions that I had to really think if I had had any special symptomatic problems on my birthday.

Directly after radiation on November 13, I was taken to ultrasound, where Dr. Dillow performed another amniocentesis. I was disturbed because the baby was moving within me. A good-sized needle was inserted in the amniotic sac, and the fluid was extracted. Dr. Dillow exclaimed that she could feel the baby kicking the needle, and I was very upset when I saw that the sample was not clear, but bloody. I thought the baby had been pierced by the needle.

Within myself, I was incensed. I refused to wait for the wheelchair service and walked back to my room. I knew the evidence obtained was important, but the means seemed as primitive as when they used leeches in medicine shows. Then my ward nurse told me how last year a fetus went into intrauterine shock when the cord was inadvertently pierced. I raged.

An order came forth for me to come into the labor room and be fastened into an abdominal belt to measure fetal heart tones. As the ticker paper rolled out onto the floor, it was within normal limits, except at random there were utterly irregular, abnormal-looking scratches. It seemed like the baby was having cardiac arrests. I took the strip back to my room. The floor doctor rested me with his words. The bloody tap was the result merely of nicking a blood vessel in the placenta. The scratchings that seemed like heart failures were ordinary fetal movement.

Machines give me screams when I don't understand.
Give me the answers in this doctors'-man land.

The view from my window, which had been my sustaining friend, turned into a great enemy. Its message was my separation from my family. It spoke louder to me each day. I would yell at the window and out of the window: "Willamette River, you may as well be the Mississippi for as near as I am to home."

The chart didn't record homesickness, but I began to suffer this malady of separation. I had never had this disorder before. I would find myself thinking of our little house with the vines growing over the front porch. There is a stained-glass window hanging over an antique couch, given to me once while I was walking to the grocery store. I spent my mind on such details.

When Dr. Mainer made his rounds in the morning, I told him in solemn tones, "I've lost my will to live," pause, "in the hospital."

On November 14, I completed 1700 rads of radiation. On November 17, the X ray showed that the tumor was shrinking. That afternoon a man whom I had never seen before came into my room to state that I could be discharged that day.

Good-bye for now, and another plastic identification wristband was cut away and disposed of.

I was put on a schedule of once-a-week visits to Dr. Mainer, who now concurred with my original due-date for the baby. It was decided to let me go full term as a result of a hematology and radiation consultation.

I had a fur coat that was once my mother's; it became my winter pleasure. One December doctor's visit Matthew hatched a plot as we waited in the examination room. He turned off the light and it was very black. He waited on his hands and knees behind the examination table. He wrapped his animal stature in my fur.

"Well," said Dr. Mainer. "What's this?" upon finding such a dark room. With a ferocious growl Matthew crawled out to attack the physician.

Dr. Mainer reached the light switch and the rest of our time was routine.

I respected Mike Mainer immensely. I was always a person-patient with him first, not just another case. This was based on a feeling, not words.

It was rare for our conversation to go beyond what was medically relevant. He kept disclosures of his inner self on a strict budget.

I was told once that the residents make twelve thousand dollars a year. That sounded like Tarzan's ivory horde to me.

When Mike Mainer told me he frequently moonlights in the emergency room, I was surprised. I knew he worked an abundance of hours as a third-year resident. I apologized for being bold and rude but suggested that free time for walking in mountains was sweeter than gold.

"Buy clothes in a thrift store for a change," I said.

He laughed but replied that school loans were due.

We left his office and went to the cafeteria. He asked me to sit with him. He was wearing a genuine World War II leather flight jacket and a "thank you for not smoking" pin. He asked me about how I had become a Christian.

I told him that ten years ago I had a single experience that was a birth into a new way of life. I was in a wooden cabin built on the back of a pick-up truck en route to Alaska to homestead.

January 22, 1967

I spent an evening in self-examination. I found the inside of myself was like a very dirty house.

I lacked the power to undo my disorder: the way I wanted to be, I was not. The way I did not want to be, I was.

I was overwhelmed and prayed in earnest for the first time. The result became a relationship with Jesus Christ. He was no longer a rock of offense, but my cornerstone.

Mike looked at me and said, "I once was a lot happier. I want to get back there again."

I increased in bulk in December. I was so pregnant that even when empty seats were available on the bus, people would spring up and offer me theirs too. I knew I would probably never have another child, and even those enlarged, uncomfortable days were put on special tapes in my mind. I only heard one line for the "Christmas Story": "And she was great with child . . ." (Luke).

My official due-date was New Year's Eve, December 31, and it was arranged for me to be induced at this time. As I left for the hospital, I gave the baby basket a last look. It had been a strange forest I had carried the child through.

Richard and the children drove me to the hospital, with the children singing all the way, "This is the day, this is the day." They dropped me off at the hospital's north door with final instructions: Matthew wanted a boy, and Anna wanted a girl. Neither cared what color the baby was.

It was standing room only in the labor room. Others must have had tax exemptions to worry about. I had to be rescheduled. I rode the bus home, glad for two more days.

Richard said, "What are you doing here?"

I said, "It wasn't the day after all."

On New Year's Day, I took the children roller skating on the sidewalk. I pulled them along and held them up at the same time. How we feel can be just like a wind of weather; I was happy. I was full of life, in me, around me, on each arm.

HOSPITAL
JANUARY 2

I went to the hospital admissions department; I called it the "booking room" under my breath. Everything in hospitals always begins with questions. By now everyone in the office seemed to know me. A nurse took me to the OB delivery and labor suite. Mike Mainer and I met at 8:00 A.M. "Good," he said, because he is a man of schedule.

My assigned labor bed was under a window, and Mount Hood was visible that day. An amniotic hook was used to break the membranes and because this might also stimulate natural labor.

Then I was surrounded and attached, plugged into and connected to machines.

The first baby born in outer space.

A fetal heart-monitor belt was buckled. An abdominal contraction belt was buckled. I had an IV, and a special box that seemed to have a green flashing light. At 10:45 they began the drip of pitocin, or "induce-juice." My body believed it and began to make contractions.

The abdominal contraction belt transmitted the tremors to a graph I could watch. It was like a child's drawing of hills on a strip that would roll out and pile up on the floor. The baby had its own paper recording its own heart.

Having once lived on the OB floor for two weeks, I had friends among the staff. They came and sat with me through labor. The machines were at my front, and my sisters gathered around my back. The floor doctor asked if I had ever been induced before. For some reason I thought he asked if I had ever been *seduced* before. We all laughed, and the humanness overcame the machines. It felt like a home delivery.

At 1 o'clock, I had dilated 6 centimeters. A scalp electrode was applied to the baby's head, and there were more wires. At 1:20, I was given oxygen through nasal prongs.

When the contractions reflected on the graph looked the same as Mount Hood, I closed my eyes. Richard came and held my hand. The contractions intensified. My sisters applied pressure to my lower back.

At 2:15, I was rolled into the delivery room and everyone came with me. Mike Mainer dashed in, just in time.

I was permeated with a sense that all was in order, and my mind seemed to expand to the universal of women having children, not in any time-space sequence, but from the beginning to the end. The baby crowned; I kept forgetting to watch the mirror.

At 2:35, Mary Elisabeth was born, instantly cried, and the roomful of adults seemed to move back a generation.

My sisters moved with me down the hall. They knocked at the nursery door, and the baby was held up. She weighed almost nine pounds. They all exclaimed in the talk of women. I felt I could run the length and breadth of the world.

I was moved into a postpartum room where one nurse delighted in pushing my abdomen. I understood the "uterus-shrink" principle, but she maneuvered as if she were in a great contest to press all the air out of an air mattress.

It was the original birthday party, and my eyes could see balloons pinned to the ceiling, and it seemed there should be cake on the dinner tray. I was given the same window berth in Hospitalization No. 4 as in my previous captivity.

Some infant formula company had given the hospital a sign which was put in the hallway, prohibiting visitors. They would wheel down the babies in long trains of portable beds.

They brought my baby for the first time with instructions not to nurse her until she had been given sterile water. Newborns are like birds puckering their faces; something's about to come. I nursed her. A mother with her infant has had to be painted by every generation.

Saturday and Sunday Mary Elisabeth was mine for a brief season, with a circle just around us, and all the cares to come had to recede.

Mike Mainer had gone on a vacation, and Steve Fredrickson was my overseeing physician. I had more than a new mother's schedule.

I thought: so short the rest, so often the test.

Monday, January 5, 1976

En route to nuclear medicine, the wheelchair driver snatched my chart away and carried it himself, not to lead me into temptation. I only wanted to distract my journey with nurses' notes, which can sometimes provide four-line comedy relief.

The nuclear medicine department has its permission forms to sign too, with their twentieth-century seal.

I was injected with radioactive isotopes so that a liver-spleen scan could be performed. One of the doctors stretched me out on a table. I could watch my liver and spleen glisten on a wall screen as if they were loaded with Mexican jumping bean gold-dust.

On the other side of the room, another patient was placed on a table and the technician took a shuttle and passed it back and forth over her body. She kept pleading for water, in a way that made the word sound like six syllables. I thought, "So this is what it's like to make a James Bond movie."

They would give me no sign of what the test revealed.

I was instructed to wear a lead apron when I held my baby. I had to use a formula for a given period of time and discard my breast milk.

1. The baby is wheeled in.
2. I have to wash with an antiseptic cloth, turning the first smell of mother into a deodorizer.
3. I'm girded with a lead apron, adding forty pounds to my postpartum weight.
4. I'm given a bottle with a whole list of ingredients . . .

5. My breasts say, "Now what's the matter?" I use a breast pump that looks like
   a bicycle horn.

Who cares? She is a healthy baby. But I want
the doctors to confirm that with me.

Upper-mantle radiation treatments were
scheduled to be resumed, and I want to know if
I can be simmered by rads and still nurse Mary
Elisabeth. A note was written requesting a con-
ference with a neonatal pediatrician and Mary
Elisabeth's mother.

In the meantime, in between time, I was
wheeled early in the morning to diagnostic X
ray for a lymphangiogram. Machines hung from
the ceiling on tracks, and I sat on a table be-
neath these mechanical webs.

I manually expressed the baby's feeding,
which seemed quite disconcerting to the technician. But she overcame her discomfiture, and
explained the lymphangiogram procedure. Dye
would be inserted through a small incision in
between my toes and channeled into my lym-
phatic system; when absorbed, the X-ray series
would show any abnormality.

The staff physician of the department came in
to view the opening procedure. I mentioned that

I had just had a baby four days ago. She asked me about the delivery, but the words she wanted to use escaped her. Instead, she made a cutting movement with her finger, and an appropriate cutting noise as a way of inquiring. I replied that I had had an episiotomy in the delivery. She rescheduled the lymphangiogram for January 13.

The neonatal pediatrician came to see me. He was the original Dr. Elevator-Driver, who pushed the button for the "photography" floor on that first real day. Stu Levy has a face one cannot fully forget and one cannot fully know because it is full of hair like the burning bush, but the flame is in the eyes.

Our second encounter is framed and hung on a wall back in my mind. In speaking of Mary Elisabeth, he said the words from the book of Daniel, without knowing it: "After examining her . . . she appears more vigorous than the rest . . ."

I felt I could levitate on the bed, and Stu asked, "Just what are you into, anyway?"

One can choke with the joy of a joke that is never said. I wanted to reply, "The American Girl Scouting Movement," but I swallowed the line.

"Jesus," I said.

He asked me if I had ever heard of Richard Alpert.

"Yes," I said, "I heard him lecture in Haight-Ashbury ten years ago. All I remember is that he admonished us to get some psilocybin, because of the realms of love to which it elevated the inner man."

Stu went on to say that Alpert had gone to India and found a ragged "holy man" who was being worshiped. Alpert wondered at this until the man revealed the secrets of Alpert's heart, and Alpert embraced him too.

Oh beggarly elements. Alpert took the wrong trail. There is one way. I am adamant. I had to hush myself, for in saying too much, nothing is heard.

I had some of the usual postpartum problems. I was constipated. In Steve Fredrickson's rounds, I shared my complaint. It took courage for me to broach such private business with Steve. Sometimes invoking the word *doctor* can pull a mask over the clinician's face; like when the imitation glasses are attached to the plastic hose with a moustache ruffle. I didn't have that prop with Steve.

MILK OF MAGNESIA

He prescribed a common, bad-tasting remedy and roused me from sleep the next morning with jokes about the medicine's effect. Often the way up is down, but I had no mental set for what I considered a delicate topic. Let self-reproach and remorse come later; I kicked his leg twice. But friends can take such abuse, where a doctor and a patient can't.

I went home that day, and he put a whole pint bottle in my medicine discharge sack.

I dressed the baby, myself, for the first time. The nurse carried her to the car. It's a state law. We carried the load of samples that all the infant-supplies manufacturers want associated with the newborn's nurture.

A song of the family is sharing the new one with the brother and the sister. Anna had triumphed in the fact that we had had a daughter.

Richard told me that she stuffed dolls up her shirt during my five-day stay. Then she would whip them out, exclaiming, "It's a girl!" to Matthew's continual chagrin. My son came and peered through all the January blankets. "Well, she looks just like a boy." So the unity of the spirit was now maintained in the bond of peace.

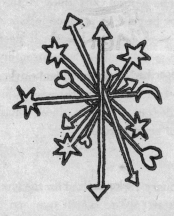

As for me, as we rode home from the hospital, I was dancing on the roof of the car, figuratively speaking.

I was not an untried mother. I fully knew that an infant takes more maintaining than just being arranged in Carter's new layette. The baby's up at night, the little children are up by day.

Sleep is an illusion, a mirage. As one attempts to act upon it, as if it were a reality, it only vanishes in trying to seize it.

I was like a robot performing every function from rote memory. It's a perfect self-denial, a baptism that can change girls to women in that exhausting underwater swim.

There were night watches when the baby would not stop crying. I often thought: The world needs a gifted chemist to put another concoction in an aerosol can. "Baby Hush" could be sprayed at bedside to produce instant sleep.

There were nights I imagined deep in my pillow I was nailing boards between myself and the sound. I would hammer planks over the wail, trying to build a quiet box to sleep in.

I wonder if a lone Chinese mother ever thought of acupuncture.

On January 13, I returned for the lymphangiogram. It's strange to watch dye and oil going through your toes being absorbed into your system. I asked how long these chemicals would be in my body. "Oh, for years," said the technician.

There was a screen that separated me from a man undergoing the same procedure. Our names were on a blackboard where the times and amounts of fluid were recorded. At random, X rays were taken to check the absorption rate. It was like we were in a contest to see who could be set free first. My feet and body ached to move, but under great penalty of loosening their devices and thus repeating the ordeal. I fell in and out of low blankets of sleep, rigid.

I won over the other contestant, and he groaned. Then I stood, and bent, and rolled, and inhaled and exhaled for the first series of X rays. It was a very strange way to spend the day; even my urine was blue.

Early the next morning the telephone rang, and I ran to the ring to keep it from sounding. I wanted to keep the children asleep, and I juggled noises with schedules to keep it all moving. But I started to bleed—filling the floor, a mess by the door.

I sat down. Matthew got up, and took in the scene. "Well, thank God you didn't do that on the Oriental rug." That five-year-old perception started me laughing.

HOSPITAL
JANUARY
14

Later that morning I had to take the children and divide them all into different houses. It's sad that the Lee family pie was again cut into pieces and distributed. There is a whole language in sighs. I felt locked into hospitals.

A medical chart is just data plus data plus data. The information from the previous tests was available. The liver-spleen report stated, "Spleen appears mildly enlarged, with a mottled liver." I didn't bend and fold on hearing this, as most medical authorities don't consider the liver-spleen scan significant in regard to Hodgkin's disease. And the lymphangiogram, which *is* regarded as relevant, was normal.

It was my night to sleep, sweet and deep. "It's my only chance," I told the nurse.

She was zealous for blood. She kept coming with a flashlight to look for stains. She was trained to read red spots like tea leaves.

It was determined that a placenta fragmentation had been retained and was discharged in the initial bleeding.

I was discharged too. I felt like a bird that had escaped from the snare of the fowler.

Hospital, hospital, number five,
one day later, I'm out alive.

I had to have the stitches from the lymphangiogram taken out of my feet. I went to the family practice clinic.

WHEN
LIFE GIVES
YOU
LEMONS,
MAKE
LEMONADE

Steve Fredrickson took off my shoes and socks. As he kneeled and bent over my foot he pretended he was a shoe salesman.

"What size shoe do you wear? What kind are you interested in today?" He waved to indicate a stockroom that before our imagination began was just a row of hospital gowns.

"Oh, I want the kind with tiny heels and pointed toes."

He acted dismayed. "Those are really out of style now."

"I know," I replied, "but they are the best for kicking doctors."

After that sentence he became a regular physician; a visiting medical student just stared at us.

I resumed the wife-and-mother hike, but I was wearing a backpack that had cast-iron pans in its sack. As an outpatient I went for treatment every day. Radiation was initiated on the upper mantle with the intent of delivering 4,000 rads in eight weeks. It was an uphill climb.

At 1 P.M., the infant, the children, and I would enter the radiation hall. The department head, Dr. Moss, once remarked, "We only see a nursing mother once every five years." Sometimes I would emerge from the treatment room to find my children darting on stools with wheel bases in between the stretchers and wheelchairs.

The path had such steep rocks. Within myself I was so exhausted that life lost all its colors, its past, and its future. I was pressed down by each day.

The radiation field was etched on my chest with red ink. Within the target area were outlines of my lungs. Lead blocks were built to protect those organs.

At home Anna took a red flow pen to make lines on her own chest to be like her mother. The children were exposed to more than I could bear myself. They played doctor an inordinate amount, making a doctor's office behind the couch. There they would take their stuffed animals to an invisible Dr. Mainer, who seemed to live back there for a while. The diagnosis was simple; everything either had Hodgkin's disease or a cold. Matthew sometimes was the physician himself. He used a chain and a lot of wet Kleenex in his treatments.

They helped my perception: *Bum thoughts could come looking for a handout.*

On the top of the hill was a veterans' hospital. It had American flags at the front entrance, unlike hospital North and hospital South.

Every afternoon a van brought the veterans over to the radiation department for treatment. They came the same time in the afternoon that I did and I knew their faces.

Greyhound bus drivers honk at each other while passing on the highway. Women with tiny children the same age smile at each other in supermarkets. The veterans and I had cancer; it put us in one fraternity.

Once I followed them through the lobby of the hospital; old men in brown-and-white striped bathrobes.

There was a murmuring behind them after they passed.

"Did you see those red marks on them? It's for the radiation machines."

It's like they were passing lepers and everyone whispered, "Unclean, unclean."

I hurried and got in the elevator with them and we all rode up to the fourth floor together.

Among the younger patients I had one blood brother named Carl, and one blood sister named Darlene. We all had Hodgkin's disease.

They were treated in the morning and if I ever chanced upon them, we would hug on sight.

I grew accustomed to the look of the radiation department. The fact that there were snowballs in stretchers who had almost finished their roll down their hill didn't make me wince. I could finally look into a melting face. It was just real.

The mothers with the sick little children were the hardest for me. They were always perfectly tender with their injured ones, who needed no tether; they didn't move.

I kept feeling a cosmic apology that mine had to emphasize the contrast of health. Anna loved to climb the coat rack to the top. The other mothers were at the other end of my tunnel.

Their child was leaving them; I was leaving
my children.

> Where are words
> That say good-bye
> I'm just going
> I will not die
> I think it best
> To shout it out:
> *See you later*
>   *alligator*
> *After a while,*
>   *crocodile.*

Sometimes due to an influx of patients or a
mechanical failure we had hours to wait on the
turquoise blue plastic couches. Matthew and
Anna would always dare a standing broad jump
and measure their flight by squares of linoleum.
The office personnel would stiffen their faces into
they-could-get-hurt looks.

Magazines became more than a turning page.
They had found all the trains and animals the
first time. They could line them up on the floor,
etching in glossy color a boat. The rest of us in
the waiting room had wet feet. Purses were fish.

The employees of the radiation therapy department were in three categories: the doctors,
the technicians who operated the machines, and
the office workers. With such a grim casualty

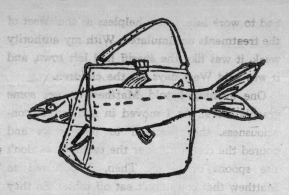

rate, they took release in celebrations. They marked staff birthdays with wild tribute to the sugar industry. They would transform their employee table into a grandiose pot-luck confectionary. I had been there so long I was ushered into their inner sweet circle. Under the influence of so many diet admonitions, it seemed to me a shocking display of sugar castles. Anna called them "yummie crummies." One doctor confided they gave him two birthdays in one year. There was never one raw cauliflower on a toothpick. *Let every man be fully persuaded in his own mind.*

My strength was breaking down into half-lives. My body was in rebellion. My lot became the baby and the couch, while Richard had to resume care for the rest of the ranch. When he had to work late, I was helpless as the effect of the treatments accumulated. With my authority weak, it was like the sheriff had left town, and it was wild West days for the children.

One evening I told Matthew to get some granola cereal. As I moved in and out of consciousness, they decided to play cows and poured the cereal all over the table. Cows don't use spoons or bowls. Then, it occurred to Matthew that cows don't eat off tables. So they poured their nutritious flakes all over the floor and ate them, mooing on their hands and knees.

What a sight to bless a mother's weary heart.

It was time to bring more authority into town. One call to my mother put her on the afternoon plane.

We were all in subjection now to the fastest gun, and order reigned. To further ease the exhaustion, my mother was going to take Mary Elisabeth home with her.

I was warned that the upper-field lung blocks were originally calculated on the simulator for my girth as a nursing mother. Thus, I could not wean the baby without threat to my lungs. I wanted my mother to stay as long as she could to keep from having to use manual expression to maintain a nursing mother's dimension. And more than that, it's very hard to see your little baby fly off to California for an unknown period of time.

But Mother had her airplane reservations and was eager to fly back to a comfortable twentieth-century house with her bundle. Besides, her girl friends were planning a shower.

We made an appointment for a complete pediatric check-out before the flight. The family practice clinic got three generations. Steve Fredrickson was temporarily replacing Mike Mainer in looking after us.

Before being ushered into the examination room, I found Steve peering through his glasses into a microscope and shared in brief my situation.

Dr. Fredrickson did such a thorough examination of the newborn. A rash and a stuffy nose elicited great concern. He asked if my mother could remain until this was stable, simultaneously giving my leg a tap.

*　*　*

A few days later I finished radiation on the upper mantle. I nursed the baby for the last time, then Richard drove Mother to the airport. Matthew and I sat and cried and hugged each other. He had decided that Mary Elisabeth was his very favorite.

The night Mary Elisabeth flew to California my friends had a baby shower for me. I opened a pile of miniature clothes which were passed around the circle of ladies.

oh, goodbye for now

We made limericks as a contest. The winner was Kate Carson:

There once was a baby named Mary
Whose days in the womb were quite scary
She had a rough time
But she came out fine
And now all the saints are so merry!

We ate cake, cutting a glazed, healthy stork into squares.

My friends were well-lighted houses where I could go and rest along my way.

Four inches of hair fell out as a result of the radiation treatments. It filled my brush; I piled it on the floor. My neck looked like someone had put a bowl on my head and shaved across. I had an inverted receding hairline. When I tried to braid it my nakedness made me look like I was wearing a cheap wig a size smaller than my head.

There had been some question among the radiation therapy doctors in regard to removing my spleen. This is a routine procedure for determining the stage of Hodgkin's disease.

The fulcrum of the consideration was in the preservation of the ovarian function, as the ovaries could be moved to midline and shielded during the lower-mantle radiation. Thus, I would not be thrust into menopause. On the other hand, it could be an unnecessary major surgery and the doctors reported certain possible problems once a spleen was removed.

I tried to manage my own decision, wading through a series of medical school generalizations. Everyone I asked had a concise laparotomy lecture. I took my question off the book-shelf and asked the faculty what they themselves would do. Again, some said yes and some said no. I entered carrying a black-and-white question and left holding every possible shade of gray.

I called Mike Mainer and packed together this great gray ball of considerations and rolled it to him. He decided on the laparotomy, and I had peace. It was nice to just be able to think in four-line poems again.

There was a very short span between the completion of upper-mantle radiation and my scheduled surgery. I would say, "Stomach, you'll never look this good again. . . ."

HOSPITAL
FEBRUARY 29

I was admitted under surgery's banner. The greeting orderly put me in a ward with four beds in a tight row. As he wrote his "white female admitted, ambulatory" introduction, he asked me how to spell "disease." The lady in the next bed was testing the smoke sensitivity device in the ceiling by keeping her hot cigarettes rolling.

"Please move me," I said. I was taken across the hall and put in a two-bed room under the window.

One of the surgery team members came in, identified himself, and began an examination. He left the room, and another man came in and asked the same kind of questions, and gave me the same kind of examination. As he left the room I thought it was odd, but when a third came with the same procedure it seemed to be very funny—and it might be very disorganized. I did not want the surgery department disorganized. But they all came back together: it was the admission plan.

I had two days before my operation. I was offered every color of jello and every flavor of bouillon cube. I fasted, and embroidered a bird on an old coat.

A hospital patient can have a multitude of roommates. A certain quality of the hospital experience is in that particular interaction. There are a lot of different kinds of animals in the hospital ark.

I had roommates so young on the OB floor that they were back in the part of the world that sighs over rock-'n'-roll stars.

I had a roommate so old the nurses and I called her gramma, and she ached in every direction.

I once thought they brought a man in to share my room, complete with tattoos and after-shave lotion. He was a she, with cancer of the uterus; she was tough by day, but cried at night.

I had one roommate who would flip her front teeth out and then draw them back with her tongue. She talked all the time in streams without reason.

There were sweet little sisters, and ladies whose years had bent them into ways that were their own.

I now had a new roommate whose legs were healing from donating skin to a mastectomy wound. Her name was Clara; she was wise and kind and clear. She had spent her years as a pastor's wife in rural Wyoming towns.

She told me wonderful stories about western ranch life, but she was quiet in quiet times too.

There are groups within groups. No one knows from where the wind blows or where it goes.

Somehow I heard of a Bible study held every Tuesday morning at seven in the hospital South cafeteria. It was led by Dr. Ritzman, the chief of staff of the cardiac division, with his wife, a doctor also. They prayed for me; they knew of my pending operation the following morning.

The head of the radiation department, Dr. William T. Moss, is a most eminent man. Not only is he a frequent speaker at medical conventions, but he has written three textbooks which have been widely distributed in schools for the study of radiation oncology. He exudes professionalism.

Once, in the hall, he quietly remarked about my coming laparotomy: "Put a tape across your abdomen and write 'ouch' on it." In that minute, we were both ten years old, and I almost fell off the chair laughing.

March 3, 1976

I was scheduled for an 8 A.M. incision. I was up very early and watched the sun rise over the hills and city. I felt at rest. My mind once tried to elbow my peace to get its attention: "Can't you be a little nervous?" But somehow I was unshakable.

I was given a preoperative sedative. It made me feel like a little child trying to stay awake, not wanting to miss anything. Somehow the ceilings received this great attention as I was wheeled into the surgery room. The anaesthesiologist who ordered the ingredients of that haze was in the room. I told him, "I am remembering everything." Those were my last words.

I woke up in a body that was not sick, but tortured. I was in a room which seemed to contain lots of people stretched out in my state. It was as if we were on a battlefield of beds and some nurse in the distance was bending over to tend the injured and wounded soldiers. The face of Dr. Ed Temple, one of my surgeons, blurred in front of me. I just moaned for him as a dying soldier would do, and went back to sleep.

What a great capacity we have for pain. My first night, consciousness was nothing but torment. There was a tube down my nose reaching into my stomach, attached to a continuing suction machine that was not working properly and had to be replaced.

The call light in our room was broken. My roommate and I shared one hotel desk bell between us to ring for aid. Clara was in charge of it.

I could not talk or move my body. I could only grab a nurse's arm and pull her close to me and whisper, "I need more medication." She replied, "You just have to expect for it to hurt." I felt utterly dependent on others for survival.

In the morning Mike Mainer came, and I told him I needed a stronger dosage to counteract the pain. He understood. He said, "It was like going

to hell and coming back." That was very pro-
found, at the time.

Morphine was my consciousness-decreasing
drug. For a while I had no awareness of the sequence of day and night. It was either dark or
light when I opened my eyes. I had chest con-
gestion and wanted to cough up a thick mucus,
but it hurt too much. My body raged with fever
in its own global warfare. I was taken on a
stretcher for chest X rays.

After one injection of morphine I had a
hallucination. A girl was weaving by my bed.
She held out strands of colored yarn for me to
see. She was gentle and I could see right through
her.

I told the night nurse and she must have told
a doctor on the floor. A very hip young medical
man put his head around my yellow curtain and
said, "Are you having a good trip?"

Somehow I began to mend in such small little
ways, I could hardly tell. They helped me get up
and walk. I felt like I was a tiny bug walking up
the wall and across the ceiling. My world began
to open to time and shifts and people.

When the doctors on family practice rounds came to see me after surgery, I had the overwhelming impression they were visiting a kitchen sink. Not only did I have a hose in my nose, but inserted in my wrist was a tube leading to a gravity-fed water bottle, and my urine was collected in a plastic bag.

Oh, humble kitchen sink, my porcelain was indeed chipped.

Friendships grow, and as they change, show their depth. Some are slow in the knowing and the growing, but last. With Dr. Cris Maranze, it was fast. We were always friends.

Cris was the family practice doctor who rotated into my surgery team after the operation.

She had very long hair. Mostly she had to twist it into rope and tie nautical knots to have a sanitary-code head.

She wore a white coat. One pocket bulged with mini prescription books of pills and dosages. The other held the tool that illuminated her hearing of inward processes.

At night she would come, and we would build ladders and attach extensions to them and climb up into ideas. In the morning she would come with the surgery glee team to ask if my bowels had moved yet.

One night she made a confidence. She introduced it by first swearing me to secrecy. I assured her I would never tell anyone and waited. She declared it was only in a best friend category that there could be such a disclosure. I waited. "My real name is Harriet and no one knows it." I never told anyone.

I told Cris how I could live on fifteen dollars a week for groceries. It was a life-style that made my mind as sharp as a stockbroker over the price trends of inseason produce. I was a merchant ship of store sales.

She wanted to know the stories of a lady at home, and I wanted to know the stories of a lady as a doctor.

Our respect was great toward each other.

I recovered into an air of comforting optimism about the findings from surgery. Everyone agreed as a group that it had looked and gone well. One of the team was a medical missionary candidate, and I nailed him alone to tell me the truth. He, too, agreed it looked good. A Christian family practice doctor confided that he had prayed for me outside the surgery door.

The staff member who dictated the operation record for my chart said under *Findings:* "The spleen was grossly normal," and the postoperative diagnosis was the same as the preoperative diagnosis: Stage II out of the four possible stages of Hodgkin's.

I rested in the confidence of my doctors. On the morning of the pathology report, I remarked that the paper would be final that afternoon. The attending physician said, "That's right, but I don't expect them to find any abnormality."

Nothing prepared me to see such a grim Dr. Mainer come in and stand by the window, and such a serious Dr. Temple enter and lean against the wall.

"I have some bad news and good news," Mike Mainer said. "The spleen was enlarged, weighing 220 grams, involved with Hodgkin's disease, consistent with nodular sclerosing. The good news is I've talked with hematology, and you won't need any chemotherapy."

Mike talked as if he were reading a paper he had typed in his mind before coming in. They were very heavy words to have to say. He left the room. Dr. Temple stayed with me.

I was stunned. I knew I must be in Stage III. I could count my thoughts and emotions, as if my head had broken into a lot of little pieces and they were falling slow enough to number. I was mad at every encouraging word and that I had believed them.

We all stood two inches tall; I was set up for a fall. It was winter, and they took my only coat.

At that moment, I could see birds flying north again. They seemed free, and I felt bound.

I had studied Hodgkin's disease. Like an examination where the answers are on a page in your textbook, I could see the survival-rate graph for the third stage. The print was too small to read, but it was a reduced residue of years.

I have three little children, not even old enough for school.

That is so searing a thought, so like an AT WAR headline that I said it out loud.

Dr. Temple took some Kleenex out of the drawer and wiped my eyes. I hate to pull people into my drama: Let them be free. So I pulled

out my defense mechanism, girded myself in its armor, snapped the visor over my eyes and asked, "How will this affect the managing treatment policy?"

Dr. Temple replied. "You will be scheduled for regular X rays and liver-spleen scans."

"But I don't even have a spleen any more."

"Oh, that's right," he said, softly, and left the room.

I was alone. What could I do with my mind? It was like I was in an elevator and my will could push the up or down button. I sang a portion from a song that a minor prophet sang thousands of years ago:

Although the fig tree shall not blossom, neither shall fruit be in the vines; the labor of the olive shall fail, and the fields shall yield no meat; the flock shall be cut off from the fold, and there shall be no herd in the stalls; yet will I rejoice in the Lord, I will joy in the God of my salvation. The Lord, My God, is my strength (Habakkuk, 3:17, 18).

The song could be turned up and sung out loud, but I could not turn it off. It was like the Holy Ghost Radio Station.

My agony turned into a great joy that was beyond understanding: And joy is one with peace. I was in a very high place, and I wanted to look around. For a brief time I was on top of an embroidery, instead of on the bottom side where the knots are and the threads cross. It was a perfect work.

I wanted the doctors to come back so I could comfort them. But instead Clara came, and she knows how to weep with those that weep, and rejoice with those that rejoice.

I fell asleep making plans to go to Dr. Ritzman's Bible study in hospital South.

Tuesday, March 9, 1976

I could walk only with great discomfort. This was a little offset by bracing a pillow against my abdomen.

105

I got an extra-large pair of men's drawstring pajamas and inserted a feather pillow, firmly joining the strings as tightly as possible. I put a long maternity dress over this configuration, plumping and smoothing, looking full term. It was my only chance of being able to cross from hospital North to hospital South. I took a wheelchair, but abandoned it shortly thereafter.

I moved slowly through the early morning hall. The corridors were vacant until I saw a doctor whom I knew only slightly.

Dr. Haley looked at me and his face turned into vaguely funny shapes. Curiosity swung far beyond politeness, and he reached out his hand to touch my stomach. I drew back quickly and said, "Almost due." "Yes," he said, "almost due."

Later, I was told, he came into the clinic and asked, "Am I going crazy, or is Laurel Lee crazy? Didn't she just have her baby?"

I made it to the Bible study. When I returned to my room I felt like a great athlete.

With an abdominal incision, joy can be a real problem. It hurts very much to laugh. Sometimes I would just try to think of the most terrible things to sober a good humor, but my comic sense triumphed.

I had conflicts with some of the nursing staff. I would wait until I really needed pain medication before requesting it. Occasionally I asked a little earlier than the prescribed interval but always within a thirty-minute reef of the allowed time. They always refused, once stating I had a mere ten minutes before it could be allowed.

The rules are made for the patients; some nurses saw it that the patients are made for the rules.

I saw another thing, too. The registered nurses were often so busy maintaining IV bottles and pills that jobs were given to the aides that were beyond their capability or their sensitivity.

Perhaps my discomfort was producing intolerant observations. Our whole situation was exaggerated by having a single hotel bell with which to summon the staff.

At home Richard was involved in a pediatric thirty-two-hour rotation. Matthew and Anna both had the influenza. Thus I could not be discharged home, but a house opened up where I had never been before. I went from the hospital into this unknown hospitality.

The family have several children, and their pictures took up two of the dining room walls. Most were grown now, and only two were left at home. I knew the mother had died of cancer last year, and I was sensitive to this grief.

They took me into a back bedroom, offering
me books to read. The stack included a maga-
zine called *Cancer Victims and Friends*. On the
cover was a picture of shiny crystals of laetrile.
Inside were reports about a Tijuana clinic and
an underground railroad to transport those in
need.

The books contrasted the nontoxic approach
to cancer, through diet and natural supplements,
with the toxic approach of radiation and surgery.

My body didn't feel well, and I had a stream
of people coming to aid me in my transfer to the

natural way. It was done out of true concern, yet it was overwhelming.

There were many voices urging me to consider my diet:

Your food shall be your medicine and your medicine shall be your food (Hippocrates, 424 B.C.).

BOOK A: Take nothing into your body that has been cooked or processed; if necessary sell the stove and buy a good juicer.
1. Give up meat immediately.
2. Give up milk in every form forever.

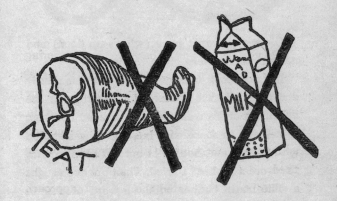

BOOK B: Only a pittance of the millions spent on cancer research has been used for nutritional investigation.
1. Experimental cancers develop

109

most rapidly on low-protein diets.

2. I have yet to know a single adult to develop cancer who habitually drank a quart of milk a day.

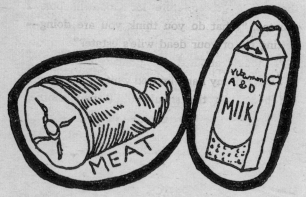

Glasses of carrot juice (what's up doc?) and natural snacks were given to me.

My host took twenty-six pills with his dinner and confided that it was a lot less than at the beginning of his treatment. He opened his chest of drawers to share with me, and it was stuffed with bottles and bottles of natural supplements. "You are a junkie," I cried. Then my eye caught a white satin banner with the word *Mother* in gold lettering. It was from a funeral wreath.

I decided to chance the flu for the night and called Richard to come and take me home.

* * *

On one of my last nights in the hospital I had spoken to Richard on the phone. He told me he had been cleaning the closet.

When I was back home I found that he had taken a portion of my clothes and deposited them in a grocery-store lot Goodwill box. I shouted, "What do you think you are doing—getting rid of your dead wife's estate?"

"I thought about that," he answered.

I had lost my hand-knitted white sweater with red hearts on the shoulder. I'll find another cardigan, I argued back in my mind. It doesn't matter.

The next day, March 14

The clouds in the Portland sky were folded together. The children and I rode the airplane up through the mattresses and drab feather ticks we were bedded under, and there was the sun above Portland. We went to California for two weeks to stay with my parents, recover from surgery, and see the baby.

I was with all my children. I was so weak Matthew had to pull me in the big red wagon to the park. But I was with all my children again.

April 1976

I had a checkup in the hematology department. It was notorious for keeping patients waiting hours beyond their scheduled visits. I'm sure we got dusty we sat so long. "Cobwebs are growing between your back and the chair," I announced.

Collectively we had the impulse to clap when the nurse finally began to call for the patients.

The radiation field is set up with delicate precision. Behind one of the CAUTION: RADIATION signs is the simulator room, where the treatment area is calculated on a large machine with a Picker brand name. I was helped onto a table next to a panel of buttons. Arching over me was a hood, looking like a large green praying mantis, with dials of numbers for eyes. Its face was square, with lines called X and Y. There was a note which read, "Target to surface 40.3 centimeters."

The table centers its patient, and the lights are dimmed as the technicians take refuge in a lead-lined room of dials. Bells sound, and you can see your bones on a mounted TV screen.

These procedures are repeated with pieces of lead string marking certain spots, and then the boundaries are painted with flow pen. In this manner I was prepared for my next series of treatments.

I took the bus with the children for the first radiation on my abdomen. Returning home, I waited to transfer buses in the downtown city center. I felt altered but not sick.

An enormous red double-decker English bus, carrying advertisements for local stores, made its way down the street. The attached sign said FREE RIDE, with a map of the circle of stores it stops at.

Of course we all scrambled up its spiral stairs to sit on the tweedy plaid seats on the top. As we turned the corners, I began to feel a low level of nausea. The bus pulled into Import Plaza and parked as the driver blithely announced that this was the end of the line today.

I was beginning to feel very nauseated and a long way from home. "I'm sick, stay with me," convinced Matthew that the merry English bus ride was indeed over. I pulled the children with me through the run-down Burnside district. Matthew was excited at seeing all the empty bottles along the sidewalk. "Let's collect them and cash them in." I said, "There's no refund on wine bottles, Matthew."

We crossed by the casual labor office, and I knew I was going to need help. I tried to call a friend, but even the print was blurring in the phone book.

I began to vomit in a garbage can. A part of my mind could feel people driving by thinking: "Look at that . . . an alcoholic . . . at her age, and such little children . . ."

A social worker from the labor office came over to me. I said, "It's not what you think, it's radiation!" He was polite anyway and directed the children and me to our bus stop. I sat and leaned against the building, instructing Matthew to watch for the Number 40.

The ride was a long-suffering journey. I knew I was going to throw up again and decided that the most unobtrusive depository would be my purse.

I became a bus-ride attention center. I was passed one Kleenex, someone opened my window, and another moved as far from me as possible. The bus driver refused my transfer as I finally rang the bell two blocks beyond my stop. I climbed down the stairs and my purse spilled all over the sidewalk. That was the journey from Hiroshima to my bed.

The medications lessened the nausea; but I was always wading through it, and I could hardly eat. I said the word *food* backward. It was now *doof* and I didn't want any.

"I am going to turn into the bones that walk." The doctors had a solemn assembly: a staff member, my radiation resident, and two technicians. I joined them. They sat straight as arrows and first suggested reducing my dosage. Then they spoke again, "We feel you need marijuana." It was unreal. All of a sudden it was like a Peter Sellers movie, and we may as well all sing together "The ballad of the busted brownie . . ."

They stopped my expanding meditation by referring to an article from the *New England Journal of Medicine*. They told me about another young Hodgkin's patient who stated that he stayed stoned and well.

Cris Maranze pitched a copy of the article to me on her way to family practice clinic: "Antiemetic Effect of Delta-9-tetrahydrocannabinol in Patients Receiving Cancer Chemotherapy."

Dr. Moss began to take a new interest in my case. I gave him the article to read, and he personally administered the rad reduction. But he didn't feel that any "extra" medication was necessary.

As my strength decreased, an empathy grew in me for old people. I suffered from many of the common geriatric problems. I had to watch other people take over jobs that in health I could do with more efficiency.

One of the continents in my mind perceives not in words, but in shifting images. I felt like I was driving around in an old junk Studebaker body, where in health I was a four-wheel-drive jeep that climbed mountains.

I was sick. I was weak. I had fevers and weight loss. I was again admitted to the hospital.

HOSPITAL
MAY 10

There were no hospital beds for females available in hospital North, so I was sent to hospital South, where I had never camped. I was taken to the twelfth floor and assigned a bed next to a young girl in what looked like a body cast. She had her television going and sang along with all the commercial jingles as I changed into pajamas. She asked me if I liked Jesse James and showed me how far she could sit up, all in a matter of minutes.

I decided not to cross the sheets with my body and went to find a nurse in the hall. I asked for mercy. It was as if I'd been hitchhiking, and was picked up by a car with a crazy driver. They put me instead in a Cadillac: a large single room

Hospital, Hospital
Number Seven
Salvation is free
then there is Heaven

with a view. I rested in bed, so grateful, feeling as if I'd won the daytime TV prize. It was quiet.

Weakness is like being in another gravity zone where there is just not enough energy for activity. I had to plan my moves.

Pictures are like extra windows, and I had none. From the pediatric floor, I chose six different quilts and hung them on the wall and put them on my bed. I took plants from the lounge

and put them on the window sill. I did all these things with the permission of the nursing staff. Then I rolled up my bed to enjoy the view.

The nurse brought me a note to sign. It read: "Consent to take full responsibility for bed to be in high position. The hospital is released from all responsibility for any accidents resulting."

There I lay all day, except for radiation.

The weekend schedule had reduced personnel and observation. My first Saturday back in the hospital, I made a secret arrangement with Stu Levy and Cris Maranze. I walked out to the main driveway between North and South and sat on the curb.

They were coming to get me for the afternoon. They pulled up in a junky white Chevrolet, the

kind of car that looks like it was born at a
drive-in movie.

Stu's hair hung down to the steering wheel.
The tassel from his high school graduation cap
(1966) hung down from the rear-view mirror.

Once Stu told me people could accept him as
a craftsman or a farmer, but not as a medical
doctor.

We went to the civic center. Stu went to an
exhibit of photography equipment. Cris and I
went to a funky junk show of neat old groovies.

I tired so fast, I could not last. I sat in a chair.
Cris sat with me there.

I took out my embroidery thread and showed
Cris how to make a herringbone stitch. She took
off Stu's corduroy shirt and built a line of teepees
in thread until we left.

* * *

Their house was in the hills by the Portland Rose Garden. On the step of their front porch was a foot scraper built out of two horseshoes.

In their library was a tree growing from a pot all the way to the ceiling. "That's Arthur the avocado," Stu explained.

Over the fireplace was a rock-'n'-roll band picture of the Sacred Mushroom boys. Stu's amplifiers stood like watchdog giants in the living room.

They showed slides of their Arizona backpacking trip.

Stu told me a special summer guest doctor was coming from New York. "Dr. Lipkin is a sage," said Stu. I visualized a Dr. Sage, who would look like he was from the Himalayas with long hair like Stu's, but solid white.

I fell asleep on their couch and they had to tiptoe around.

It's not me, it's just my body that acts like this.

I started to write my hospital journal, but I could only create a skeleton of experience with words.

Help is just somebody else's plan for you. I had a phone call from someone I did not know, who gave me the address of Dr. Contreras and

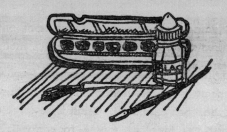

his laetrile clinic in Mexico. A lady brought me two books advocating laetrile. They were too late. I was too tired to read them.

In the shower one morning I found more swollen lymph nodes in my groin. A biopsy was scheduled with Dr. Temple to determine if the malignancy had spread.

I talked to Richard and he spoke such a graphic phrase that I had to walk around it very slowly.

"Have you ever seen two dogs and one has been hit by a car," he said. "The other just walks around it and howls, not knowing what to do."

The night before the surgery I wanted to write. I went into a doctor's small office on the floor, because it had a desk and chair. A medical student was there, wearing a baroque parquet-floor tie and reading three books.

One was a jumble of crazy images, never coming to any conclusion, but nonetheless having power to play tag with the mind. It was called *Even Cowgirls Get the Blues*: "The brain that pound and a half of chicken-colored goo, so highly regarded (by the brain itself), to which is attributed intricate and mysterious powers, that slimy organ (it is the self-same brain that does the attributing). The brain is so weak that without its protective casing to support it, it simply collapses of its own weight. So it could not be a brain."

It's a new generation of doctors and mailmen, but the bankers always seem to remain the same.

Biopsy Day
Friday, May 21, 1976

It wasn't an early priority surgery, but it was to be done before noon. I decided the lymph enlargements were guilty of disease and had to be proven innocent. In this attitude I could have no letdown from pathology. Only the pubic hair on the right side was removed, and I was given enough medication so that I would be relaxed during the incision procedure.

The first effect of the narcotic was that I began staring at a quilt that I had mounted at the foot of the bed, becoming wrapped in its design and color.

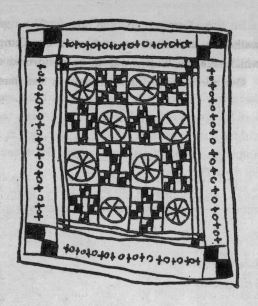

In this state of mind I was taken to the surgery floor, hospital South.

First I was wheeled behind a curtain, where one other girl was also waiting for her scheduled room and hour. Between us was a baby in a crib. The girl kept talking to the baby and would ask me or any passing nurse if we were the mother. I just thought she got more dope than I did. Then I was wheeled into surgery and transferred to the table. I was draped except for my face and entire groin area. Above Dr. Temple were two large lights that seemed like large bug's eyes, but not of a menacing species.

In this X-rated position, the staff surgeon walked in, looked at me, and asked Dr. Temple which side the biopsy was to be performed on.

Our minds can bring forth data in less than a second. I was immediately reminded of my first biopsy, when all the betadine preps were done on the left of my neck and without comment the node was removed from the right.

So I sat up on the table, looked at the staff surgeon and said, "The side where they shaved."

Then it was obvious that it was a dumb question. The nurses and doctors looked each other in the eyes, but the surgeon's position prevented us from laughing. It was one of those little moments common to all, where the emperor in the parade discovers he has no clothes on. We were the only two that had spoken, and without another word he left the operating room.

Dr. Temple made the incision. I could feel the blood run down my thigh.

Mike Mainer once shared in detail how a cesarean section is performed. I remembered all the steps and began to abstract. I allowed free play in my ideas and decided I was having a minute cesarean and was going to give birth to an infant the size of my thumbnail. I slept the rest of the afternoon.

* * *

A hematologist examined me. He had a closet of pet lions, and his recommendations unleashed several for my contemplation. Their mouths were open.

"Although she is still, clinically, in Stage III, the severity of the symptoms makes more widespread involvement a possibility. Because of this, chemotherapy (MOP) is in order. Normally, patient would be rested four to six weeks, completing radiation. However, because of the aggressiveness of the disease in this patient, that time may not be available. We are waiting staffs' opinion as to this.

"Suggest:
1. gallium scan
2. bone marrow
3. bone scan
4. liver scan
5. liver function test
6. surgical consultant for biopsy of inguinal mass"

These lions stayed in my room. At times they were very big, and I would tremble. Sometimes they were small, but they were always present, with teeth.

The biopsy report confirmed the spread of Hodgkin's. There were days to wait before Dr.

Bagby and the staff returned from their convention. It was a time for me to consider the possibility of chemotherapy.

Dr. Ritzman sent a friend of his with fourth-stage Hodgkin's to my room. He said the only reason he was alive was chemotherapy.

But once Dr. Hood had said, "I've killed people with chemotherapy."

One text wrote, "Significantly, the sites of major toxicity of these chemotherapeutic agents are not all the same: Although most are myelo-toxic, some primarily affect the nervous system or gastrointestinal tract" (*Cancer Journal for Clinicians*, December 1975).

Besides the concern of the cancer-causing agents, I did not want the top of my head to look like my knee. A disease and its treatment can be a series of humiliations, a chisel for humility.

My room had been an ice-skating rink. As I sat and wrote, I glided through the hours, leaped over barrels, and was exuberant.

Now there were holes I had to maneuver around. My feet could get wet and cold, and I would shiver on the bed.

I had an official pass for a weekend afternoon. I asked Richard if we could take a ride in the country. I was starved for landscape. I got dressed but he never came.

I felt like a sociology documentary I once saw of the unwed mother. Often she vests her expectations of security in a boyfriend who never comes to see her in the unwed mothers' home.

Later I reached him by telephone and he said he had taken Matthew, Anna, and some other children hiking.

The same weekend Mike Mainer asked me if I would like to go for a ride with him.

I asked Richard and he said it was a good idea. Mike had a small German car with a window in the roof. We drove west through sloping farm fields. One meadow had a track of red flowers like a solid letter spelled into the earth.

"It's clover," I said.

"It's not clover," said Mike.

He backed up the car to settle the horticultural question. It was a crimson clover variety.

We waded out and I lay down in the scarlet verdure. It reminded me of when I was a child in Illinois and we would make imprints of angels in the fresh snow. We would wave our arms and legs into wings and dresses.

"Mike, there really is a Heaven," I said.

"I can't believe that," he answered.

"If we stood back in history three hundred years and I brought you a report of a continent I found with animals so different from those on your farm, you wouldn't have believed me then, either."

We ate tacos in a drive-in. We went back to the hospital. I shared with him one square of my worry about Richard's attitude toward me.

"Stay as close to him as you can," Mike told me.

Friends arranged to bring my children for a few hours. I was so excited. I went up to the pediatric floor and walked past the wall mural of Snow White into the game room. I explained to the volunteer that I wanted to borrow some toys and I would bring them back. I filled a red wagon with mechanical wonders, stories, and dolls. I took the stars and left the cast of thousands.

I got a bowl of crushed ice and little bags of a crunchy kind of food.

The children came; ever moving, ever talking bursts of energy. They had a style of appearing to explode into an infinity of perceiving parts. We flowed together.

When they left I was so exhausted I could hardly move or speak. I wanted to remove the toys. A sadness permeated my being. Maybe all the storybooks had sad endings. I hit the wrong floor button and wandered around, a stranger pulling a crazy wagon in her nightgown.

As I slept a nurse took the cloth wrapping off a sterile instrument. He smoothed out the material. He painted with a blue flow pen a moon face with wide eyes and an enormous crescent smile.

He climbed over my bed. He climbed over my plants and hung this banner down from my window, using the extra-wide masking tape.

It was the first thing I saw in the morning.

The day came when some of the hematologist's six recommended points would stick me. They were planning to do a bone marrow. I waited.

The hematology staff chief had returned; he came into my room with Dr. Bagby and Mike Mainer. He said he was not convinced that chemotherapy or any of the tests were at all necessary. The inguinal nodes were an untreated radiation port, thus their enlargement did not mean I had had a relapse. His recommendation was a discharge from the hospital, with a further course of radiation on an outpatient basis.

He took every lion with him. I roared for joy. I wanted to tear up that first hematologist. As Mike Mainer left the room, he told me to "Love thy neighbor as thyself," and closed the door.

LOVE THY NEIGHBOR AS THYSELF

On my very last day, a man came and introduced himself as the technician who once gave me a barium swallow. "Look," he said, "these are the stains on my pants when you spit out the drink."

I took down the quilts, put the plants back and went home.

Thursday, May 27

Home is said to be the one place you can go and they have to take you in. If I'm a rock thrown in the water, home is one of the first rings from the weight. It is you in things.

I walked into someone else's house at my old-shoe address.

The living room was not the grandmother lace card where I once read *David Copperfield*. Now there was a television set against the wall.

I had only allowed the kitchen counter a line of antique cans. Now there was a beach of practical kitchen movement: A silver toaster had its electric-cord hand under a blender umbrella; an electric can opener was wearing a green plastic bikini; tacky vendor stands of canisters advertised "flour" and "sugar."

"This is how it's going to stay. I couldn't find anything," said Richard. "And that stove," in-

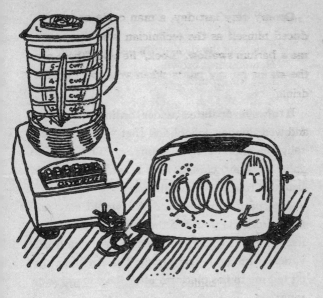

dicating my blue enamel queen on her ornate throne, "has to go. It makes the pans black."

So I walked through the house and the floors were slanted uphill.

Friday, May 28

Richard took the children to the baby-sitter.

Saturday

He helped the baby-sitter take her dirty clothes to the laundromat. She was a young girl raising two children alone and her car didn't work.

Sunday

This was the day my house fell down.
Remember it brown,
Like the ground.

I always operated under ordinances. I was allowed Sunday school and that was my formal religious training time boundary. The children went to their classes and I sat in the back, listening to adult admonitions.

The pastor's wife asked if I would stay and share from the pulpit in the main service. It was like a new application of working out my salvation with fear and trembling. An elder escorted me to the platform after the congregation sang:

Storm clouds will come
Strong winds will blow,
But I've got a Savior
And He's sweet I know.

The faces spread out before me. There was a television camera for the auxiliary room. It's a large congregation.

I made paragraphs. I left the rostrum. I left my Bible. I left the church. I was tired.

* * *

Richard took the children hiking. It was raining and they were wrapped in blue nylon zip suits. His last words were, "The fire will go out in three hours."

The pastor's wife came by with my old ragged-flag Bible. She brought me a new one with large print and references. The elders had signed it. I paraphrased their message to "keep on trucking."

Richard never came home. It was night. *If I were a mouse in a cold old house, what a cold old mouse I would be.*

I called the baby-sitter. They were there. They had all gone hiking together.

Thoughts flew around in my head. I understood that to him I was dead.

We talked that night. "We're in two different kingdoms," he said.

How can two walk together unless they be agreed? The feeling of love that promotes tap-dancing down supermarket aisles, leaping over bushes, catching blooms between the toes; that goes. But the fact of love becomes a code of behavior.

"Love suffers long, and is kind, seeks not its

own, is not easily provoked." But there is only rest when every eye stays in the nest.

As I put the children to bed late that night, they leaned out of their bunks built from plate glass packing crates to sing. They had Sunday school songs. They pounded their fists one on top of the other and the lyrics ran:

The wise man built his house upon the rock
And the house on the rock stood firm.
The storm came up,
And the rain came down,
And the house on the rock stood firm.
The foolish man built his house upon the sand
The storm came up,
And the rain came down
And the house on the sand went squish ...

They spread out their fingers and sang it again.

Monday, Memorial Day

Friends opened houses to me. Richard started to file for divorce.

The Wade family was a cloud of dew in my summer heat. I had my radiation series to slug out and I slid each night into their home plate. They gave me their bed, and they slept on the couch. The Wades had two little girls. I watched the family well and long; they were sound.

140

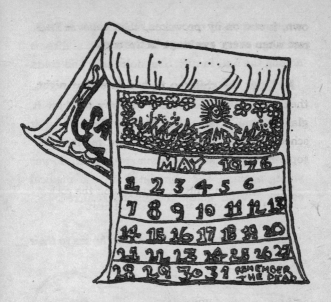

I ached in concern for my children. They came to visit me. It was a comfort that youth could be so insulated by their merry hearts.

I was in the wilderness of my life. I was a Gretel without a Hansel lost in the woods. There was a wicked witch who would eat me if I would listen. *In my thoughts were my wars fought.*

Weeping may endure for the night,
But joy cometh in the morning (Psalms 30:5).

I rented the upstairs of an old house. I turned each window into a greenhouse. The children came home. Anna played Maple Leaf, a child's interpretation of the words *make believe*. There was no more outbreak of Hodgkin's disease among the doll family. The dolls only had colds.

I finished my journal. I was shy to show it, but I gave it to Mike Mainer. From him it passed in and out of the residents' mailboxes.

I had my last radiation treatment. I was young again. I had completed all the medical course possible unless the disease recurred.

In Oregon, the salmon run from the sea to their

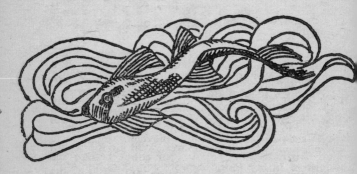

spawning ground. There are nets. There are sporting men. There are rocks and ascents so steep some die from the journey itself. But some silver salmon make it home. It's a matter of percentage; it always is. I could grow old.

* * *

My last treatment was the very day family practice clinic had a farewell dinner for its graduating residents. We ate on the roof in the sunshine.

Stu could only grab a hasty plate, as he still had tables up and down the hall to serve, like a Dr. Waiter.

I pretended that I was graduating, too.

The head of family practice put his arms straight out to the side and said, "I'm an airplane."

"I'm a cloud," I said, and he hugged me.

I met another guest in the hall, Stu's sage, Dr. Mack Lipkin from New York.

After that day Stu called and organized a videotape session with Mack Lipkin and myself.

Dr. Lipkin came into the studio reading my book. He had his thumb on the page where the breast pump looked like a bicycle horn.

Stu cared more about our comfort than the clarity of the recorded picture. He dimmed the major illuminating lamps to reduce the heat.

I had borrowed a copy of Mack Lipkin's book. He's an authority in his field, and has served as a consultant to the Surgeon General. I shared one of my favorite paragraphs, where Dr. Lipkin was speaking with the head of a major medical center. He told him that he thinks it should be required that every graduating doctor first produce a bowel movement in a horizontal position with three witnesses present.

"Is that right?" asked Stu.

"Yes," said Dr. Lipkin.

Dr. Lipkin asked me to come to his office the following Monday at nine in the morning.

After an eclipse, the sun emerges from the shadow.

One morning a man from church came to my door and offered me a scholarship to Bible school.

Friends contributed to buy me a round-trip airplane ticket. It was a vacation in a box addressed "to Mexico for Laurel." The children were to go to their grandparents' house while I traveled south.

Monday, July 26, 1976

I had to hurry to make my appointment. I rushed out into the early morning street and waited for my bus.

An antique store had been closed for a long time. This was the day they were loading the furniture into a large rented truck.

"Oh," I sighed, knowing I should wait for the bus, but I entered the shop. The owner sold me a wooden cuckoo clock for a quarter. I turned its face into my dress so it looked like I was only carrying a large birdhouse.

The owner went and stood on the curb, overseeing the hoisting of his furniture pieces.

I saw the orange bus at the top of the hill. "Look, I didn't miss it at all."

The proprietor emerged again and gave a gift to me. It was a rich leather book called *Blessed Be God*. The pictures were in such hairline detail they could be printed into religious paper money.

* * *

I entered Dr. Lipkin's office on the third floor of the family practice building.

He said he found some charm in my book and asked to send it to an editor friend in New York.

I felt like I was a very homely girl who someone thought could be in a beauty contest.

I jumped up and down in my chair and somehow this activated the clock in my lap. It went "Cuckoo, cuckoo" over and over until I thought I was flying over the cuckoo's nest.

What could I give Mack Lipkin, wise sage, great doctor? I had a little sketchbook of watercolors I had made of passages in Thoreau's *Walden*. I ripped out a favorite page: "The essential laws of man's existence do not change just as our bones are indistinguishable from those of our ancestors."

My book went to New York. It was like a piece of paper a child floats out into a stream. It was soon out of sight. It will get caught in some weeds, I thought. There are holes in it. It will fill with water and sink.

But I lifted up and flew on.

Afterword

I was in a very firing squad of circumstances, and there in my hospital bed I experienced the peace that is beyond understanding. Even though my outward frame was perishing, my inward spirit was being renewed day by day. As my joy increased in Christ, so did my burden that others might know Him.

The original book was written for four student doctors. I had shared with them that Jesus was "the way, the truth and the Life." That He loved them. That He had died for their sins. That He was alive today and that they could know Him. The book was in essence a very personal and intimate tract, hand-bound and illustrated. I rolled it, I packed it tight. It was a little snowball that began to roll away from me with a momentum that was beyond expectation.

One student doctor shared the book with a summer staff member. He in turn mailed it to New York where a publishing house accepted it for publication.

I am thrilled with the truth of the Scripture. "Nothing is impossible with God." Truly all things are to work together for good for those that love God and are called according to His purpose.

LAUREL LEE